OTHER BOOKS
BY KATIE CAREY

Available on Amazon now:

Soulful Poems: Heal the Heart and Soul

Entangled No More: Women Who Broke Free from Toxic Relationships Building Their Own Empires

Evolving on Purpose: Mindful Ancestors Paving the Way for Future Generations

Soul Warrior: Accessing Realms Beyond the Veil

Intuitive: Knowing Her Truth

Evolving on Purpose: Co-creating with the Divine

Coming soon:

Becoming the Manifesting Diva: Creating Ripples While You Flow (Now open to receiving applications)

Soulful Poems Vol 3 (Now open to receiving applications)

Evolving on Purpose (Vol 3): Akashic Journeying into Wealth Consciousness (Now open to receiving applications)

Visit https://www.soulfulvalley.com

DISCLAIMER

The publisher and poets are providing this book on an "as is" basis and make no representations or warranties of any kind with respect to the book or its contents. The publisher and the poets disclaim all such representations and warranties of healthcare for a particular purpose. In addition, the publisher and the poets assume no responsibility for errors, inaccuracies, omissions, or any other consistencies herein.

The content of this book is for informational purposes only and is not intended to diagnose, treat, cure, or prevent any condition or disease. You understand this book is not intended as a substitute for consultation with a licensed practitioner. Please consult with your own physician or healthcare specialist regarding the suggestions and recommendations made in this book. The use of this book implies your acceptance of this disclaimer.

The publisher and the poets make no guarantees concerning the level of success you may experience by following the advice and strategies contained in this book, and you accept the risk that results will differ for each individual. The testimonials and examples provided in this book show exceptional results which may not apply to the average reader and are not intended to represent or guarantee that you will achieve the same or similar results.

This is a work of creative nonfiction poetry.

SOULFUL POEMS

A GLOBAL COLLABORATION OF POETRY
TO HELP YOU TO HEAL AND GROW

POETS

KATIE CAREY   AILISH KEATING   CASSIE BROOKS

CATH LISTON   DESIREE ANDERSON   FIONA BLACK

GILL KIRKHAM   HAIDEH KHATIBI   HELENE RAYE

JOS POUNE FAE   JULIE CROWDER   KAREN COLQUHOUN

KATE SMIT   KATHERINE CRESSWELL   KATIE BOCK

LAUREN COLLETTI   LAURIE JONAS   MAC McGREGOR

PIPPA MOSS   PRITI HATHIRAMANI

TANIA FOX   VIVIAN SHAPIRO

SOULFUL VALLEY PUBLISHING

TABLE OF CONTENTS

Other Books By Katie Carey iii

Disclaimer iiv

Introduction 1

AILISH KEATING 3

   The Rush 3

   Reflection 5

   The Sun 7

About the Poet 8

CASSIE BROOKS 9

   Forward Motion 9

   Introspection 10

   Progression 11

About the Poet 12

CATH LISTON 13

   The Visitors 13

   Travelling to Nine Mile 15

Kiss Nose Cuddle 18

About the Poet.. **19**

DESIREE ANDERSON **20**

Tides of Destiny... 20

Lessons of Love 22

About the Poet.. **23**

FIONA BLACK **24**

This Is Me 24

Freefall.. 25

About the Poet.. **26**

GILL KIRKHAM.. **27**

The Cosmic Truth... 27

About the Poet... 30

HAIDEH KHATIBI **31**

Stillness 31

About the Poet... 32

HELENE RAYE **33**

What If.. 33

About the Poet 35

JOS POUNE FAE **36**

I Do Not Apologize 36

About the Poet 38

JULIE CROWDER **39**

Little Girl 39

Anger 41

Coma 42

About the Poet 43

KAREN COLQUHOUN **44**

I Am Her and She Is Me 44

About the Poet 47

KATE SMIT **48**

She is here 48

The Angels Said 50

She speaks 52

About the Poet 54

KATHERINE CRESSWELL **55**

Hearts Desire 55

About the Poet 56

KATIE BOCK 57

Warriors, Witches, Women 57

The Illumination of Darkness 59

If Only… 61

About the Poet 62

KATIE CAREY 63

Traumatised 63

Co-creating with the Divine 65

Habits and Resolutions 67

About the Poet 69

LAUREN COLLETTI 70

Not on the Dollar Menu 70

About the Poet 71

LAURIE JONAS 72

A Beautiful Life 72

A Simple Message About Life 73

From Confusion to Enlightenment: A
Transformation Story 74

About the Poet 76

MAC McGREGOR 77

Birth of a Cloud 77

I will not go away. 78

The Star 80

About the Poet 82

PIPPA MOSS 83

My Feet are a Portal 83

About the Poet 85

PRITI HATHIRAMANI 86

That Ten Percent 86

About the Poet 88

TANIA FOX 89

A Time for Grief 89

About the Poet 92

VIVIAN SHAPIRO 93

What do I do with my King Size Bed Now? (October 1994) 93

Ramblings about Life While Sitting by a Pond April 2021 96

On Tears 100

About the Poet 101

About the Publisher 102

INTRODUCTION

Welcome to the Soulful Poems Series! I am thrilled to introduce you to our second book, which takes the form of a Poetry Collaboration. In this book, we have brought together a diverse group of Healers, Coaches, Authors, and Poets from all around the world. Each contributor has poured their heart and soul into their poetic creations, resulting in a collection that is truly inspiring and thought-provoking.

As you delve into this book, I encourage you to open your heart and mind to the profound connections that can be made through poetry. Whether you are seeking solace, inspiration, or a deeper understanding of yourself and the world around you, I am confident that you will find poems within these pages that resonate with you on a soulful level.

To enhance your experience, we have included an "About the Poet" section for each contributor. This provides you with an opportunity to connect with the talented individuals behind the words and explore more of their creative works. By connecting with these poets, you can further immerse yourself in their unique perspectives and artistic journeys.

I hope that this book becomes a cherished companion, offering you moments of reflection, comfort, and inspiration whenever you need it. May the poems within these pages touch your soul and remind you of the beauty that can be found in the power of words.

Katie Carey
Soulful Valley Publishing

AILISH KEATING

THE RUSH

What's all the fuss
The constant rush
The rush from here
The rush to there

Catch that plane
Jump on that train
Catch that bus
What's all the fuss?

Why is a day no longer enough
Has the hour shrunk?
And faded away
Like time
It was never here to stay
Just borrowed
Yet even with all the rush
It's still not enough

We are energy efficient and

Sleep deficient

Technologically advanced

Physiologically enhanced

Emotionally starved and

Psychologically scarred

And still, we rush

To catch that bus

To nowhere

REFLECTION

Like a deer caught in headlights
I was stunted by your gaze
All at once, naked
Vulnerable
Wide open

You must know what you do to me
When you strip search my soul
You know everything about me
My past, my future
You know
And then you look away
Leaving only my indifference in your eyes

For what am I?
Human, flesh, pride
I have nothing to hide

I scratched my chin
And wondered
Was I dreaming?
It all happened so fast

Then I gasped
It was happening again

So I return your stare
Reflecting like a mirror
Blinding your indifferent eyes
And then I look away

THE SUN

The birds take the time each day

To wake us

Without consideration for themselves

Dutifully, each day

Their songs reach our ears

Dawn takes the time

Each morning to slowly and gently

Reveal The Sun

The Sun reverently approaches each day

Breaking gently and slowly

Upon our horizons

The flowers awake to each day

Gently unfolding their petals

To greet The Sun

All in a daily ritual

And what is ours?

How gently and reverently

Do we greet each day

Following the pattern of nature

Or following the grid of man

Allowing that breath to resonate

With the birds

Allowing our bodies to stretch

Like the horizon

And unfolding like the leaves

Allowing our lungs

To reverently

Breathe The Sun,

Our Fire into existence

And upon seeing each other,

Bringing and breathing

Each other into existence

ABOUT THE POET

Ailish Keating is an International Best-Selling Author. A talented Soul Guide, Healer, and Hypnotherapist, she empowers clients to embrace the present moment for a more fulfilling life. Ailish leads transformative journeys, both within the soul's depths and to sacred locales in Ireland and Egypt.

Connect with Ailish below:

Ailish.com

FORWARD MOTION

Let it happen.

Let it flow.

Let it go.

Enjoy the ride.

There's no rush.

The world is yours to experience.

It calls to you.

It speaks to you.

It moves you.

Walk your path.

It is your journey to discover.

You will learn a lot as you go.

You will outgrow a lot of things.

You will lose parts of yourself.

But Daughter,

O but Daughter,

You will find yourself.

You will be free.

Let it happen.

Let it flow.

Let it go.

INTROSPECTION

Stop.

Just let it be

And just be.

Look within

And remember.

You will see.

Know your light.

Embrace your darkness.

Tinted windows -

A stained-glass masterpiece.

Your beautiful essence

Realigned,

Connected to your Source.

We are one Daughter.

Continue your sacred journey.

Choose love.

Choose peace

And trust yourself.

Look within

And just be.

PROGRESSION

In the plane drawn between space and time,

You feel the presence of the ancient ones hall.

Sacred whispers call to you from the abyss,

Recesses where few get to tread.

Listen to the words of old but speak not of hidden things told.

One day a Priestess of court you will be,

But your glimpses are not for all to see.

Trust the wisdom imparted to you

And stand not in the shadows of those you wish to follow.

Work with them if they allow,

But words spoken in vow are truer made.

Live and let live,

Allowing what is yours to flow naturally.

Grit and grace is your creed,

So work hard and blessed you'll be.

Extend the net for others to yourself as well.

You are no different than they.

No better. No worse.

A conscious collective are we,

And what's done is three times three.

Seek the heavens and the moon.

Watch my creation on display.

It speaks freely if you choose to listen.

One spirit, one life born through many ages.

You are a walking universe,

Creating life with each breath.

Breathe deeply, Child.

You're on your way.

Don't judge yourself too harshly.

Each step moves you forward into a new day.

Keep moving until your journey's end

Only to begin again.

ABOUT THE POET

Cassie Brooks is an Award-winning Children's Author, mom, and LBGTQIA+ advocate, driven by her mission to inspire and empower young readers. With the release of her picture books, Cassie shares her belief in the importance of embracing one's unique self and not allowing others to define who we are.

Connect with Cassie below:

https://www.facebook.com/cassandra.weaverbrooks?mibextid =ZbWKwL

CATH LISTON

THE VISITORS

The visitors are leaving now,
They've been here for a while,
But they've outstayed their welcome,
By a country mile

They were never really welcome,
But I felt I had no choice,
It's hard to kick visitors out,
When you do not have a voice

It started small, but as it grew
Their presence became all,
And what pieces of me that were left,
Became scared, alone and small

Their stay was filled with anger,
Shitfuckery, lies and pain,
Although I tried to make them leave,
The stain of them remained

As the words pour out of me,

And splash across the page,

They carry all the toxins, the vitriol and rage,

And all the words I wish I'd said,

When I was forced to cower,

Flow out from me now…

I speak my truth…

And I am filled with power

I TAKE BACK my house now,

And evict them from my home,

Send their filthy attitudes packing,

Fill my soul with what was lacking,

And breathe the sweet air of victory,

As I see,

A brand new me

The visitors are gone,

There's still some tidying to do,

Now my home is clean and fresh and new,

I know what I will do,

I'll drink a toast to the me that's here,

Those visitors were really rough,

Cheers and here's to knowing,

I am

And I'm enough

TRAVELLING TO NINE MILE

I know where my final journey will be,

When my feet no longer roam,

It will be out to the Nine Mile,

To the red earth, my living desert home,

Where my ashes will float on the breeze at will,

Cast from the hands of the ones I love,

It's all part of living your life,

As old as the earth, and the sky above

A journey that starts from now,

Because yesterday is gone and done,

And whatever happened, doesn't matter,

What matters…… is yet to come

What's yet to come are all the things,

I've put off, for another day,

I'll start doing them,

Make it happen,

For life is short they say

Plan that trip to new lands,

To the mountains with ice and snow,

And other places I've dreamed of going,

But was far too busy to go,

Take our pets and Destiny to the beach,

Smell the salt and sea,

Sleep to the rhythms of the waves, breathe slow, and deep and
free

And plant those veggies, herbs and flowers,

To make an oasis garden grow,

Feel the earth between my fingers…

The smell of earth and water lingers….

I will reap the harvest that I sow

Laugh with all my loved ones,

And have them share a meal,

Pour the wine, eat the cheese,

Savour the joy I feel,

They're here because they love me,

Such times are a precious gem,

For the love that comes back to me…I'm giving out to them

And I want to be a guiding hand,

Showing others the way,

To find their truth, and understand,

A peace inside…… that's there to stay

And I'll make time to be still,

To hear the birds,

To deeply sigh,

Notice music in living,

Feel what natures giving

I know whatever comes my way,

I'll be strong and not afraid,

Things don't always go as planned,

That's not how lives are made,

And though I know where I'm going, its fate that decides the way,

I'm ready, smiling, holding tight, as I travel day by day.

The journey that has been my life,

Still has a way to go,

It's a validation, celebration, of everything I know,

Of all the things I'm yet to learn,

In this wondrous life of mine,

I'm humble, and I'm sure,

That everything will be fine

KISS NOSE CUDDLE

I knew this day would come
But I thought it would be far,
When our darling Anna girl,
Would leap out from the car
Grab her things, her hat and bag,
And be off on her way,
Bye Grandma, she gives a wave,
You have a lovely day

No more kiss, nose, cuddle

Confident and self-aware,
Bag on back she walks away,
Without a backwards care,
I love to see her happy,
And skipping off with glee,
Kids will grow, things will go,
That's how it's meant to be........

ABOUT THE POET

Cath Liston is a wife, mother, grandmother, and creative who dabbles in Art and Poetry. Cath is a Clinical Hypnotherapist with her own business, Catalist Wellness, specialising in trauma healing. Cath loves all things woo-woo and spiritual, all things with hair and four legs, and growing her outback oasis garden.

Connect with Cath below:

www.catalistwellness.com

DESIREE ANDERSON

TIDES OF DESTINY

I swam across the ocean
Searching for fame
Wondering if I'd ever see
My loved ones again

I was mesmerised by the beat
Of my ancestors' drums
They said:
"It doesn't matter,
We are One"

The sun of a thousand days of summer
Have warmed my skin
I've loved
All of the places I've been

In the autumn of many seasons
I've watched my dreams collide
With wisdom and love
I navigate the tides

I've faced so many fears
Weathered pressure and pain
Through the winter of my tears
I've drowned in my own rain

I've been reborn
On the oases of spring
I celebrate my wins
I'm evergreen

The past still washes over me
From time to time
Old memories haunt me
Like shipwrecks of fermented wine

My legacy unravels
On my life's travels.
Through the oceans of my mind.
I'm falling
I'm rising
I am DIVINE

Can you hear me calling?
You can become all you're meant to be
Connect in synchronicity
And embrace your Destiny.

LESSONS OF LOVE

I'm writing to tell you that I'm fine
Many years have passed
And I wonder,
Do you think of me from time to time?

I've learned to love me
Wholeheartedly
The aspects of myself that need work,
are loved too, unconditionally.

It was tough to start again
Looking at photos from back then
I see the brokenness
I recall the lion's den.

I'm finally whole
I've found myself a home
I've gathered up my skirts of shame,
I've unpeeled the layers of my soul

I've released the beggar that longed for love
I've let loose the hurt from being betrayed
The demon of low self-esteem is slayed
You'd be amazed

I wonder why our stars collided

Ending in a catastrophic sunset of fire

If I could have it again,

I'd give you a wide berth

To dominate in your own separate universe

I'm writing to tell you that I'm fine

I've gone beyond the childish nursery rhymes I'm like a

symphony that's reaching its crescendo

Thank you for the lessons from our time

ABOUT THE POET

Desiree Anderson is an International Best-Selling Author, Master level Coach, Speaker and Founder of Crest Coaching & HR. She helps heart-led, ambitious, and creative clients ride the crest of a wave and reach their full potential in life and work.

Connect with Desiree below:

www.crestcoachingandhr.com

FIONA BLACK

THIS IS ME

On one particularly beautiful morning

When the timing was ripe

She unfurled her precious petals

Allowing for the whole World to see

The most intimate parts of herself

She had been keeping hidden

And as she stood there shining

In her full magnificence

Neither shrinking away

Nor boasting her beauty

She whispered softly to herself

"This is me"

FREEFALL

When the old comforts of the mind fall away
And you find nothing but emptiness beneath your feet

No ledges to stand on and nothing to cling to
Just wide open space
The illusionary sense of self is terrified by the abyss
And it tries to grab onto anything it can
To feel safe
To feel comfortable

This is when you face your ultimate fear
The fear of your own death
Yet this is not the death you think it will be

This is the death of all that is False
And the birth of all that is True

Authentic you
Undivided you
Whole you

A you that is not superhuman
But more earthly human than ever before

Free falling is not a choice of the mind
But a deep yearning of the Heart and Soul

It's a deep surrender to the wisdom of the Universe
And a free falling into the arms of grace

Let go into the free fall my friend
Your true freedom and liberation is found here

ABOUT THE POET

Fiona Black is a Healer, Channel and Midwife for the Soul. She works with powerful women changemakers who are ready to claim their gifts and to be seen and heard as the revolutionary leaders that they are. You can find out more about Fiona and her offerings and

Connect with Fiona below:

www.freedomwithfiona.com

GILL KIRKHAM

THE COSMIC TRUTH

The oceans are profound; the seas will rise.

Now is not the time to despise,

the eloquence of those who speak

their truth

Your choice is your own to stay aloof

Dimensions open; awakening unfolds

the pressure is on; to fit into a mould

The entangled distraction of rabbit holes,

confuse the gentle whispers of the new soul

Self-love is the name of the wiser game,

No shame in chaos, though lengthy is lame

Sleepwalking characters become architects

As their eyes open wide and they ride the effect

The polarity dissolves as still point is found

Break the rearing horse, no more circles around

Feel emotions and voice them as you see

What do you desire? Focus and let it be!

Truth becomes joy if the voice is free
Ask for help and support, and let it be me!
Express fully every part into the light
From the riggers of judgement
from those stuck in plight

Be open to the oceans, the ripples, the waves
Hold integrity firm in your sacred space
Be available, dear ego, for perspective to shift,
Prove innocent before guilty for awareness to lift

KNOW that your heart feels actual proof,
Innocence sees distraction before
mastering the truth
The track to discernment, the rocky hill path
Climb back post fall and stand tall and steadfast

What feels correct in the moment feels like home,
Like the adventure of releasing to atone

The truth is there is no right and wrong
Don't get this, and never feel right to belong
Everywhere and nowhere all at the same time
Until this is embodied, continue to rhyme

The rhyme out, create waves, in universes,
Speak into existence often what a voice curses
Through the power of the mind manifest freely
To empower learn the simplicity of alchemy

Sit crouched down with feet in the mud,
connect to all dimensions and choose to love.
Owning truth in every given moment.
Knowing the filters, karma is the atonement.

Here to find joy and navigate the dark
The need for more is the best place to start
Be open and honest and rid harsh judgement
Gratitude in authenticity is the best compliment

The true experience is life is like the ocean
Shine light respectfully in the dark to reveal the motion
The soul know the way in every scrumptious moment
Connect through the heart, no need for atonement

ABOUT THE POET

Gill Kirkham is a profound healer, coach and facilitator who helps change makers on their spiritual awakening journey with extraordinary energetic, emotional and financial growth.

Connect with Gill below:

www.gillkirkham.com

HAIDEH KHATIBI

STILLNESS

The summer breeze carries me to the top of the bamboo trees,
where eagles fly.

It takes me over the endless fields of wild flowers
where honey is
but a flicker of a dream
in the bumblebees' eyes;
and where
the spirit of the earth,
gentle and soft,
runs through my veins.

In the stillness, I become one with all that exists.

ABOUT THE POET

Haideh Khatibi is a Reiki Master and an amateur reflexologist who has retired from corporate life and embraced her love of reading and writing poetry in English and Persian. She enjoys long walks in nature, gardening and studying old and new spiritual literature.

Connect with Haideh below:

Haideh.Khatibi@gmail.com

HELENE RAYE

WHAT IF

What if
Our verses, like a guiding light,
Leads others towards a future bright?

What if
The power of our joyful grins
Helps others to have more wins?

What if
Our laughter ignites a spark
And mends souls once torn apart?

What if
Our voices, like a symphony's embrace,
Stirs hearts, leaving a lasting trace?

What if
Our brushes, with colours bright,
Paints masterpieces that bring delight.

What if
Our dance, with moves so free,
Invites others to find their glee?

What if
Our "crazy" idea inspires
And a new way transpires?

What if
Our way heals wounds unseen
Reigniting the dream?

What if
Our dreams, like a phoenix, rise high,
Unleashing wonders that touch the sky?

What if
Our love, like a guiding light,
Leads lost souls out of the darkest night?

What if
We all believed in the might
Of the magic within us, day and night?

What if
Together, we unite,
And make possibilities ignite?

What if

United, we all choose to share,

Kindness and laughter, everywhere?

What if

Through our actions and deeds,

We sowed love's seeds and met all needs?

ABOUT THE POET

Helene Raye wants to ensure everyone knows that "The Universe Needs You." Her mission is to be a guiding light for those envisioning a life filled with love, purpose, and playfulness. She helps people rediscover their playful spirit and heal from within, creating incredible journeys of self-discovery and transformation.

Connect with Helene below:

https://theuniverseneedsyou.com

JOS POUNE FAE

I DO NOT APOLOGIZE

I make no apologies for having suddenly and quickly changed so much

I do not apologize for projecting my deep and infinite reflections onto you

I make no apologies for becoming what I was ultimately destined to be.

I don't apologize for putting aside the one I never really was

I don't apologize after all these years for finally finding me

I make no apologies for making myself my priority forever and ever

I make no apologies for facing my fears to be anchored in lightness

I do not apologize for the trials that I took on without victimizing myself

I'm not apologizing but I'm proud of every print left by my shoes

I don't apologize for being happy because that's how I decided to be

I make no apologies for being amazed at the simple sight of a sunset

I don't apologize for loving myself because for too long I
hated myself

I don't apologize for falling because each time I got up alone

I do not apologize for being misunderstood because I was not
born to justify myself

I don't apologize for being different because I no longer want
to follow this society

I make no apologies for thinking differently because my life is
now much more beautiful

I make no apologies for laughing harder for each of the joys
that pass through me

I make no apologies for being an earthly angel who dances
with wings wide open

I do not apologize for disturbing you because it is wonderful
to love yourself LOVE myself

I make no apologies for being a rebel, I am a woman of fire
and proud of it

I make no apologies for accepting myself and I encourage you
all to do the same

I don't apologize for being awake because I'm really not sleepy
anymore.

I'm not apologizing ever again because the more I breathe, the
more I love myself

Love each other as you are to the top of your beautiful souls
Like the phoenix which is reborn from its ashes, be the spirit
which honors its flame

HERE AND NOW

I promise myself to be the most beautiful story for each of my remaining moments

GREAT GODDESS OF MY PALACE I CHOOSE TO LIVE HAPPILY FOREVER AND EVER in the present moment

So be it

From my soul to yours AMEN

ABOUT THE POET

Jos Poune Fae is an International Best-Selling Author - Spiritual life coach - Self-love advocate - CEO of LunaStar Magical Fairies - Shadow healer -Darkness to light brand certification -Akashic Records - blueprint report – Lightworker - holistic therapist - Reiki Master - Mystic therapist - artist collaboration.

Connect with Jos below:

http://lunastarmagicalfairies.myshopify.com

JULIE CROWDER

LITTLE GIRL

To the little girl who cried all night
We're all grown up now, and everything is alright

You didn't realize the reason you were here
Why would anyone choose to live in so much fear?

The lessons we learned made us wise and strong
So many layers of damage, we still have to unlearn

Your bright blue eyes with so much hope
Throughout this lifetime we've learned to cope

You deserve your dreams, time to play and imagine
These things were stolen from you at such a young age
But now I give you the time to play

So, let's take the time now to dance and sing
Smell the flowers and see beauty in the little things

The love you've always desired is just within
You are a part of an amazing source and have always been

Your true perfection is hidden by life's jaded lens
You're part of the universe and a shining star

Little girl now you understand how truly wonderful you are

ANGER

The anger inside

Has been building for years

So many days

Of too much fear

I sat in the darkness

And hid my own light

Without your support

I fell into my plight

The anger grew

Within my heart

I wish I spoke my truth

From the start

My opinion never mattered

Or so my ego thought

The resentment inside me

Went right to the heart

The anger being released

Is daunted with fear

Will my truth disappear?

The explosion of feeling

Could implode the whole world

So much self-judgement

Of my inner world

COMA

Since I opened my eyes
Dazed and confused
I've been fighting to get
Back to you
The little girl who was hidden
Most of her life
The voice that went unspoken
As it dimmed her light

Year after year
Trauma and pain
Wondering what day
I'll truly go insane

But still, I keep fighting
To let my light shine
Help other people
Who the world has been unkind

Each step that I take
Has shown me my strength
The gift I've been given
Is my inner peace

Knowing the power
Of our inner thoughts

Has brought me inner healing

I could of never imagined

Who knew a coma

Could be such a blessing

About the Poet

Julie Crowder is a
Transformational Alignment Coach, Channel, Master Empath
and Shaman from Bellingham, Washington. Her current focus
is Lighthouse Moments where she manifests her true purpose
to guide others on their spiritual journey toward inner healing
and self-discovery. Julie embraces the power of the written
word through poetry.

Connect with Julie below:

FB:@LighthouseMoments

KAREN COLQUHOUN

I AM HER AND SHE IS ME

My spiritual journey is just beginning
Learning and growing, not losing nor winning
Gaining knowledge, becoming connected
It's way more exciting than I ever expected

Goosebumps galore from head to toe
I listen and wait; she's there I know
I'm her and she's me, crazy but true
She's there within me in all that I do

Guiding me gently, nudging and winking
Where am I going, she has me thinking
Trust and let go, I hear her say
Not rarely, nor often, but every day

I'm part of you and you of me
Close your eyes, I'll help you see
Your path is here, you're on it now
Forget the what, the where, the how

Have faith and follow with love and light
I'm always here but out of sight
I love this me you cannot see
For I am her and she is me

My Greatest Gifts

My greatest gifts were sent to me
To teach me a thing or two
To teach me that it's good to be
And not so much to do

To teach me that it's ok to ask
When things don't make much sense
To teach me that it's ok to stop
And sit upon the fence

To teach me that when things are tough
It's fine to take time out
To teach me that I can be heard
I never need to shout

To teach me that I'm not perfect
And neither should I be
To teach me we're all different
And there's joy in being free

To teach me what it really means
To know and love and trust
To teach me it's not easy
But surrendering is a must

To teach me that they too are here
On a journey that is theirs
To teach me what it really means
To inherit and be heirs

To teach me to believe
That the Universe has our back
That's there's more to giving and living
A life of limitation and lack

I'm grateful for these gifts
They're my absolute pride and joy
I'm blessed to have you both
My darling girl and boy

ABOUT THE POET

Karen Colquhoun is on a mission to empower mamas to put themselves first, so that they can be, do and have more! She has had several poems published and just recently published her own guided journals for busy mamas. Karen became an International Best-Selling Author with 'Entangled No More'.

Connect with below:

https://www. facebook.com/karen.cummings.568

KATE SMIT

SHE IS HERE

Inwardly, she sat

She sat with the confusion

With the uneasiness

With that which no longer fit

She could feel it coming

The change

The rebirth

It came with grace

It came with ease

And there was no longer a need to push

Inwardly, she sat

In comfort

In acceptance

For she was meant to be at this point in the game

There was no landing here by mistake

And there was certainly no moving forward without

appreciation of being here -

here now…

Here now, where all infinite possibilities reach up to meet her knowing.

Here now, where following what 'should be' done is no longer enough.

Here now, where hiding away so nobody sees is an easy out.

She
is here
now.

THE ANGELS SAID

And the Angels said,

"We've got you.

We see you.

We know the essence of your Soul.

We see your beauty."

And she felt a tear flow down her cheek
For she once saw this beauty too
It was vibrant
It was worthy
It was joy

"Oh yet it still is", whispered the Angels.

"We will not leave you.

We will not give up on you.

We are always with you."

Her furrowed face turned up a smile,
For she knew the Angels saw her worth

And deep down, she did too.

But it hurt
It was hard
It was scary
It was sad

"It's time", they said

"Time to uncoil your wings - to rise again."

"It's time", they said

"Time to reach within - time to begin again."

"It's time", they said
"Time to choose the life - the life you wish to live."

And she rose.

She rose for her -
For the little girl within
For the pride
For the love
And the Soul within.

SHE SPEAKS

She Speaks

Pause

Breathe

Listen

Feel

She shares wisdom so potent, so aligned

And when you hear her you may wonder why,

Why you did not take more time to -

Pause

Breathe

Listen

Feel

Yet with patience she will always wait

Now and then by your side

Periodically scattered within

Waiting for your call to realign again

She is there

Yearning for you to -

Pause

Breathe

Listen

Feel

She awaits

She is here

So go, go now

And gift yourself time to -

Pause

Breathe

Listen

Feel

By virtue of grace

With knowing and faith

Your Soul - she speaks.

ABOUT THE POET

Kate Smit is an intuitively led poet whose words often flow from Source. Kate likes to refer to her work as 'flow-etry'. She has a passion for guiding women in removing physical and emotional density from their body, so they can connect closer to heart and Soul.

Connect with Kate below:

soulintent09@gmail.com

KATHERINE CRESSWELL

HEARTS DESIRE

What does your heart desire?
To what dreams do you aspire?
We are guided by our feelings every day,
trust them wholly come what may.

Those butterflies showing us excitement
and goosebumps when we're aligned and ignited
Find your passions and turn it on
When it feels so good it can't be wrong!

Be led with your heart, let love lead the way
When you lean into love you'll not be led astray
So do what you love, let the momentum grow
Show the world what you know

We all have so much to offer the world
You have a story to be told
The more we share, the more we grow
We learn together and from that new seeds are sown

Follow your heart and follow your dreams

Shine your light like a thousand sunbeams

ABOUT THE POET

Katherine Cresswell is a mother of two beautiful children, here to help inspire and spread love! Katherine is a Wedding Planner, Celebrant and Wellbeing Coach.

She creates beautiful bespoke celebrations using poetry and helps people plan their very special day with lots of love and support along the way.

Connect with Katherine below:

www.instagram.com/savvyweddingsandwellbeing

KATIE BOCK

WARRIORS, WITCHES, WOMEN

Do not mistake silence for acceptance.

Do not mistake lack of action for obedience.

As Claire Fraser would say…

I am not the meek and obedient type.

Processing.

Feeling.

Observing, listening and storing information.

For the inner warrior is alive.

When the time is right,

The warrior will show.

Not with fists or fear.

But with fiercely wielded facts and empathy

To shine light upon the illusions grown from shadows

Warrior.

Witch.

Woman.

Do not underestimate the power within.

For it is stronger than you realize

With strength beyond the imagination.

Warriors.

Witches.

Women.

Not one but one of many arm in arm.

You will not burn us at the stake.

For we are powered by divine light.

Birthers of life.

Co-creating with source.

THE ILLUMINATION OF DARKNESS

Look outside the window

See beauty, see joy

Colors alive vibrantly blooming…

Outside the window

Trapped is where I am

Jailed in this dull numb box

Wanting for life

Yearning for freedom

Hoping for discovery

Yet I cannot move

Wake up, wake up

Why won't you wake up

But I am awake

Just feeling

Feeling the darkness as it bleeds through me

The shadow as it envelopes me.

I am moving through the waves of the deep dark sea

Fighting the waves as they crash.

Pretending, avoiding, sinking.

I surrender.

I allow myself to move with the waves of darkness.

Float in and out of the shadows…

I begin to see the light that flickers.

Just as the sunlight sits upon the edge of a shadow,

I must choose to step into the light,

By walking through the darkness.

Illumination liberates the soul.

The light is not absent.

The beauty is not gone.

This is just a time to explore,

To transform,

To grow.

 For darkness will always teach the power of light.

IF ONLY...

If only I could be.
If only I could see.
If only my mind would hush.
Yet life is chaos.
Forever moving.

If only peace could be found.
If only there was more time.
If only, if only, if only.

But peace is not missing, only absent from me.
And time is an illusion...
As vast or restricted as I believe it to be.

So, no more if onlys.
For I cannot change the outside circumstance.
Instead, I create peace within and move through chaos.
I choose to breathe.
Discovering the vast possibilities in each moment.

ABOUT THE POET

Katie Bock is an International Best-Selling Author, Creator of the Illuminations Card Deck and Host of the Living Free & Fulfilled Podcast. She combines her knowledge in yoga, meditation, energy work, trauma-informed care and mindset to create containers for empowerment, transformation and growth. Katie strives to support women to rediscover their power, intuition and magic.

Connect with Katie below:

www.katiebock.com

KATIE CAREY

TRAUMATISED

Traumatised by childhood
Traumatised by Life
Traumatised from being
someone's daughter, someone's wife....

But what if all that trauma
Could lead you somewhere new
To a life you've only dreamed of
Taking you from feeling blue.

Maybe that trauma served you
in some mysterious ways
Maybe it gave you strength
To stand up tall and be brave

The truth is we're all traumatised
We all lose someone dear
Death it does surround us
Traumatising us each year.

Death is part of nature
It's all a part of life
In spirit they still surround us
and want us to let go of strife.

So let's enjoy the time we've got
Let's laugh and sing and play
Let's go create more joy in life
And love another day.

CO-CREATING WITH THE DIVINE

Do you know you're a magical human,
Who can co-create with the Divine,
If you stop, breathe, connect, and just listen,
Your genius will come through, if you open your mind.

It is easier than you have imagined,
You don't have to keep pushing so hard.
Lean back and trust your inner being,
It's safe now to let down your guard.

You've been gifted but really don't know yet,
Just what you are capable of,
Feel into your magical feelings,
They'll flow through when you're open to love.

Connection is what you've been missing,
Connecting with all that you are,
That magical, gifted great human,
Don't you know, you were made up of stars.

The universe is waiting there for you,
You're not disconnected at all,
When you will trust your intuition,
You'll never be able to fall.

So stop and feel into your guidance,
And what you can go co-create,
It's waiting for you deep inside you,
It's time that you opened that gate!

HABITS AND RESOLUTIONS

Our habits they can support us
Or lead us to an early grave.
What habits can we change today?
We could use this day to be brave.

Our brains are wired against us
Our habits they are locked in
But we can create some new habits
And replace the old ones within.

When we're not being consciously aware
These old habits, they are still there
In the oldest part of our brain
Waiting for the moment we forget to care.

The path of Evolving on Purpose
Is one that we could decide to choose
Because if we live life in automatic mode
In life, we'll only lose….

Ourselves to past addictions
The misery and the pain
And it wouldn't be very long
Before we go insane.

Let's focus on the good stuff
That we could do instead
That will keep us on a mindful track
Our habits can be self-led.

While you're looking at the New Year now
And creating those resolutions
Before you set yourself up to fail
Think about mindful solutions.

We can remember that we are enough
Don't let our inner critic lead
Be gentle, kind and loving to ourselves.
We'll be far more likely to succeed.

ABOUT THE POET

Katie Carey is the MD of Katie Carey Media LTD, the founder of Soulful Valley Publishing House and the Soulful Valley podcast. She is an International Best-Selling Author and Poet. Katie collaborates with spiritual entrepreneurs supporting the elevation of their creations. With a passion for mental health and emotional well-being, Katie aims to support individuals through her multi-author books, Podcast episodes and Poetry.

Connect with Katie below:

www.soulfulvalley.com

LAUREN COLLETTI

NOT ON THE DOLLAR MENU

He sunk his teeth into my flesh

Biting my neck, licking his fingers

He told me my skin tasted sweet

And indeed, his lips did hit the spot

But he consumed me like he hadn't eaten in days…

I don't want to be somebody's quick fix

A drive through, fast food, easy way out

Because they only call when they're starving

But go as soon as they finish

And after they're done…

Well, they never want seconds

I need someone who wont leave after they've had their fill

I want someone who doesn't desire solely my breasts, legs and thighs

But all of me

Someone who comes back time and time again

I crave someone whose not hungry nor half empty

But somebody who's already full

ABOUT THE POET

Lauren Colletti is an all-but dissertation doctoral candidate. She holds a bachelor's and master's degree in psychology. Lauren has published 5 poetry books and plans to move on to autobiographical self-help. As a trauma survivor, writing has helped her recover. She hopes to inspire and help others with her authenticity.

Connect with Lauren below:

www.lmcolletti.com

LAURIE JONAS

A BEAUTIFUL LIFE

A beautiful life is one where I get to live and wake up each day, not knowing how I can impact the world.

A beautiful life is one lived in nature, seeing all the beauty that is around me.

Exploring new places and finding new trails or paths.

Discovering beauty around the world—seeing all that God has made and appreciating the simplicity of life.

A beautiful life is one where all humans acknowledge that we are part of a whole; there are no divisions among people; we are all one.

Where everyone is treated with kindness, respected for their opinions, and learns from each other.

In a beautiful life, I help others who have less. I freely share my talents and use them to spread joy around the world.

A beautiful life is one where I can look for opportunities to make someone else feel good and beautiful.

A beautiful life means being grateful at every moment that I am alive and well and have manifested the life of my dreams.

A SIMPLE MESSAGE ABOUT LIFE

You are a beautiful soul, one that is unique and yearns to break free!

Break free from guilt, judgment, anger, limiting beliefs, and fear.

You are a blessing to everyone; continue to be a light and a beacon.

Shine your light on the world.

Share your ideas and insights, what you are learning, and how you make the most of this life.

Love with all your heart. Yourself, your family and friends, and the strangers you meet every day.

You have time to do the things you love; keep figuring out what that is. Don't live life on autopilot; go out and discover what brings you joy and happiness.

Dream about a life filled with happiness, take baby steps to get there, and let the Universe meet you with infinite possibilities!

Know that you are loved unconditionally, and you do not need validation from anyone else.

When life becomes a challenge, change your perspective.

Know that there is light on the other side.

You are exactly where you are supposed to be right now, at this moment. Savor the path that brought you here.

You are a beautiful soul.

Life is a journey; make it marvelous!

From Confusion to Enlightenment: A Transformation Story

There was once a confused follower.

They weren't sure what they wanted in life.

They lived each day doing what everyone else expected of them.

Not questioning the beliefs that were handed down from generation to generation.

Living the life they think will please others and make them look good.

But they would see others doing things differently and wonder if there was more to the life they were living.

Is it possible some of the expectations I'm following aren't necessary?

Is it possible some of the beliefs I live by aren't true?

Maybe life doesn't have to be hard.

Does anyone else care what I do?

The confused follower starts to be aware that their life could be fun and joyful. They don't have to worry about what others think because those judgments have nothing to do with them. That happiness should be what they are striving for, not the pressure of looking and feeling like everyone else.

But how does the confused follower change their ways?

By becoming an enlightened creator.

By being aware and understanding that they create their life with their thoughts, feelings, and beliefs, and by being aware of and changing those thoughts, feelings, and beliefs to create a life they love.

Getting clear and letting go of the beliefs and expectations that don't make sense anymore.

Sitting in silence and envisioning their happiest life.

Do whatever small thing they can to move toward that life and let the Universe clear the path.

Be aware that happiness is always available to them, and believe it's true.

This life is too short for the confused follower to continue to live unhappily. It's time to become an enlightened creator.

To live their life doing the things that bring them joy and not apologizing for being the unique soul they are.

One more enlightened creator is finding clarity, shining their bright light, and leading the next confused follower into happiness.

.

ABOUT THE POET

Laurie Jonas is a creative writer on her blog, Living Marvelously, where she shares ways for you to unleash your marvelous potential. She wrote the book *The 5 Ls of Living Marvelously* and is an Infinite Possibilities Certified Trainer and Spiritual Coach.

Connect with Laurie below:

https://livingmarvelously.com

MAC MCGREGOR

BIRTH OF A CLOUD

Suddenly

Out of the Blue

A white form

Appears

Blurred at the edges

Gently

Billowing

Into

This world

I WILL NOT GO AWAY

I will not go away.

I hear what you say.

I've heard it before.

I am still here.

I will not go away.

I've been in that treacle you want me to tread.

The mire that is fear and doubt and dread.

There's no way out you cry from afar.

Give up, give up and curl up in your bed.

You're too young, you're too old, too ill, too slow,

Not good enough is another brick you want to instil in my head.

It's stuck, stuck, stuck in its groove.

I hear it time again, and again and again.

It's now heard with deaf ears.

Muted 'cause I know.

Been there.

Done that.

Don't you know?

Said with no understanding of

Being there yourself.

Why is it impossible?

Have you tried and failed yourself?

Failures are a chance to learn.

Licking wounds, a chance to heal.

I'm human just like you,

With a tool kit around my waist.

Just like you?

I hear what you say.

I've heard it all before.

I am still here.

I will not go away.

THE STAR

The star - to me - is a symbol of hope.

Stars: they shine brightest in the darkest of skies.

No matter if they are hidden by day; cloud, storm or rain.

They are there; in their cycle of light, - waiting -

Waiting; to shine forth, their rays of hope, on you.

Shining. Albeit from where you are, a merest speck.

Imagine through a telescope.

A journey into space.

Your inner eye will plainly see.

How vast stars appear, the closer they become.

Now hold that image; and step, inside, the slowly, rotating, orb.

And once within; bathe, in its warm, luminous, glow.

Letting troubled feelings; ebb away.

Replacing them, with flowing thoughts of your desires, unencumbered, by fears.

Clearly: from imagination to reality, your search may find; lest a fantasy it remains.

Hope, despite the odds and circumstances,

Instead of despair, procrastination, or paralysis; takes courage.

Courage: to seek, the how and why, and what and where and when, to discover your dreams.

Strength: to be your own best friend, fair critic, and to relegate any bullies within and without.

Encourage these or others of that ilk, to enlighten your way.

Brighter; the earth looks when the sun shines.

Let's zoom through the clouds, down mountains and valleys' through the streams, to the seas, and beyond.

No matter what route you take, what obstacles you meet.

May your choice of transport, lighten your tread.

You may not reach the deepest depths, but; have paddled in an ocean.

You may not reach the highest peak, but; have climbed a local hill.

You may not reach the limits of the universe, but; have flown around the stratosphere.

The wisest among us surely know; it is not your destination that's important,

It's enjoying - where possible - the journey itself.

So congratulate yourself, for each, and every, thought and action; each step, towards your goals.

Remember then, in your darkest moments, and share with me, a symbol of hope: the star.

ABOUT THE POET

Mac McGregor is *The Angelic Mirror,* an artist, soul guide and alchemist who helps clients explore their true selves by breaking down conditioning and barriers. Together, we uncover layers that obscure their authentic being, aiming to discover who they truly are.

Connect with Mac below:

https://www.facebook.com/macaroonbar

MY FEET ARE A PORTAL

My feet are a portal

To the Divine

For connection and pure love

To open, they need

Patience and loving attention

And intention

And encouragement

And movement

And space.

Then, they yield...it's so beautiful!

Softening, expanding, yawning open

Awakening, blossoming, in readiness to receive.

The heels surrender

As the Earth rushes up

Energy enters and

Fills up my cup

The tips of the toes
Pitter patter in play
The arches tingle
And show me the way
Dancing with the Earth
Every time feels like rebirth

The inhalation is the invitation
Bubbling up like a fountain of light
The exhalation is the relief and release
Soothing my body and soul into peace.

And the golden glow
Settles in my heart
Ignites and resides there
Spreading it's radiance everywhere.
Everywhere.

ABOUT THE POET

Pippa Moss is the founder of *The Radical Self-Care Movement*; her passion being working with mothers to prioritise their well-being on a physical, mental, emotional and spiritual level.

She runs a wellbeing studio in Bedfordshire, offering mind, body and soul work through yoga, massage, retreats, coaching and energy work.

Connect with Pippa below:

www.spacewithinstudio.co.uk

PRITI HATHIRAMANI

THAT TEN PERCENT

Do you know that phase, that time,
When your life feels stuck, in limbo?
When shame bullies you into hiding?
When you can't even reach out for help?

Because you don't want to hear, yet again,
How well you are doing, how brave you are;
Because their empathy actually hurts, for
How can they ever know your "rock bottom"?

"When you hit bottom, the only way is up."
 Yeah, right! What good does that do,
When you are caught in the whirlpool,
When you can't see up, down or any way?

These last few years, you have learned,
You have allowed in teachers and tools,
You practice daily, you find your balance,
You even feel good, 90% of the time.

The truth is you really are doing good,
You really have got this, for 90% of the time!
Many would say that's better than most.
Sure! But what of the dark empty 10%?

That 10% which is so real you feel frozen,
It leaves you feeling raw and ragged,
Treading along the jagged edge of nothing,
Your voice dried to silence in your throat.

They say, in that 10% lies your true power.
It rings true. Yet, truth or mere fantasy?
How do you tell the difference, when
That 10% has messed with your brain?

Answers, I have not. Just know this -
Alone, you are not. There are others
Who have walked, even crawled, this edge.
Many allowed a shift - from coping to thriving.

So, maybe just maybe...
A good solid 90% maybe,
A maybe bordering on certainty,
So will YOU! So will I!

ABOUT THE POET

Priti Hathiramani is in the process of embracing and expressing her divine soul self in tandem with her human self here on earth. This ever-evolving journey is evident through her platforms of joy - photography and poetry. She is an eternal optimist and bounces back into the light over and over.

Connect with Priti below:

https://www.instagram.com/mudinourbloodfamily

A TIME FOR GRIEF

There is a time for grief, for my head to hang, to walk with
only bones covered by skin to hold me up, my insides are
dissolved, only silent whispers in my head to chastise, lest I
wake a memory too painful to bear,

A time for remembering, when I can be alone to sob so
violently into the cavernous void I've come to know,
accepting the searing of pain through my stomach as
punishment for my misdemeanour,

To ignore life, to retreat, to bury the shame of grief, to try to
hide my fear, I did not love them enough for them to stay – or
worse, they did not love me enough to remain,

They have gone, and I cannot reach them, they are out of my
grasp, they slip through my fingers, the grief drips like molten
lava from every pore, thick, heavy, it burns, but I persist as I
deserve the pain,

The grief is hard, and I swallow it whole, it cuts like a rock
gashing my throat from the inside, words I can now never say
are silenced in my mouth and escape through the wound,
wasted, never to be heard,

I look at people who laugh and think, don't you know what's happened, how can you glitter and smile and dance, when my world is shattered and broken and has no strength,

I long for them, just one more glance, a touch, the sound of them, soothing with reason to explain why they've chosen to go, a chance to say farewell, for one last look into their gentle eyes,

And time goes on, I rise, I breathe, I learn to smile - different now, forever changed, the grief does not go, it changes shape, colour, thought and scent, but it still walks beside me – day by day,

And yet, as grief walks with me, I walk with it, I ask and learn, more about me than it, trying on forgiveness, tailoring loneliness, moulding acceptance, contemplating the adversary of death,

The days become less shrill, early bird song recalls beauty and not nails on a chalkboard, someone does something nice for me and I can cry in appreciation of a beautiful deed, separate from grief,

Some rise as you fall, so they are tall enough to hoist you out of the god-forsaken place that you have put yourself in, those people are angels, forever friends, they hold part of my heart,

And so I begin to understand, my heart heals just enough for me to trust that not everyone will be taken away, some will stay - the scar only visible and weeping to those I choose to share my inner journey with,

I have reclaimed my place in the world, I know my worth –
but – my worth is less, being less than I was, now having been
separated from you, my scales are short, the needle broken,
but still…

When we speak I hear you clearly now, in my head, with the
absence of suffering, or alcohol, or self-hurt, not the absence
of grief – for that can never be, but the absence of suffering –
maybe,

I endeavour to share my journey now, trying in a small way to
rise, so that I can grow tall enough to hoist someone out from
their own godforsaken place, through grief we come to know
each other, and ourselves,

I recognise the familiar glimmer of pain behind the eyes of
someone, and that glimmer of hope - and know I have the
privilege of love, and they have the same. And we all, still,
have the privilege of loving others.

©Tania Fox 2023

ABOUT THE POET

Tania Fox is a writer, Reiki Master and Holistic Therapist who helps people and animals increase balance and peace. She is especially honoured to work with any souls experiencing grief and loss, holding a space for them as they navigate a different perspective in life.

Connect with Tania below:

www.animalgrace.co.uk

VIVIAN SHAPIRO

WHAT DO I DO WITH MY KING SIZE BED NOW?

The trouble with being single now
In a monster king size bed
Is where do I sleep, now that he's gone
Do I buy a double instead?

The forbidden land is to my left
I'll prove that I'm alright
I'll force myself to move over there
Where I'll sleep the rest of the nights

For that's where everything is you see
The alarm, the radio too
The Kleenex box, the telephone
What else am I to do?

I'll cover his spot like he wasn't here
I'll pretend it's all mine now
Though it's different and odd and not quite right
And a true sleep it does not allow

And to top it off my feet are so cold
I better put on my warm socks
That my friend knit me for winter nights bold
To wear when my feet are in shock

Comfort's not mine over here on his side
Maybe the middle's the spot
I can then spread out maybe left maybe right
Will I ever sleep? Probably not!

Back to my usual side, I'm undone!
Good thoughts please fill up my mind
Like the fact that I can read until one
And the duvet is strictly all mine

Tomorrow I'll dig out my teddy bears deft
Especially the Steiff growing thin
And dress up the bed in the land to my left
With my friends with their permanent grin
And a rose, a fake rose I'll place twixt them all
And maybe a good book or two
The domain will be mine and I'll have a ball
Until I find somebody new!

Two Months Later and a Different Rhyme Scheme

The rose is still within its space

Self help books here and there are placed

My little corner is still reserved

For my body sleeping tightly curved

There's room enough for 3 or more

But now I ask myself: What for?

I simply love my bedtime space

When I wake up, it remains in place

Thus making a bed is so much easier

So I can get ready a whole lot speedier!

Six Months Later

I gave in to my son but reluctantly

To get Stussy, our dog, some new company.

So now along with my Husky so dear

Is Sandler so sweet, to give Stussy some cheer.

A collie shepherd, he is thin and long

The two are great friends as they get along.

Sure, my king size bed is the place they love best!

And at night they spread out from the east to the west.

Now the stuffies are gone, my books on the floor,

And I love their presence, they do not snore!

I feel comfy and safe and they keep the bed warm

As I sleep through the nights in my 'cool' bedroom dorm!

RAMBLINGS ABOUT LIFE WHILE SITTING BY A POND

Sitting on the bench by the big pond

30 times the size of the one in our former backyard.

This one resides in the valley

over which our new condo looks.

A new life now.

House sold.

Cottage sold.

Darling dog passed on.

Time to travel.

And time to rest and contemplate

sitting here by the pond.

Contemplate what?

Nature simulating life.

Life itself.

What next?

I ponder over the pond brimming with koi and goldfish,

lily pads, fountains, pond flowers, rugged rocks.

The beautiful sparkling turquoise necked mallards

proudly skim across the ripples

waiting for the females of their species to fly in

so they can show off and strut their prowess and beauty

and claim their mate.

Funny how it's the males that outshine the females

in most of the animal world,

but not ours,

For today, we all try to shine our own beauty

not only from without

but from within.

That's what counts.

The spring sun shines brightly

on this early April morning.

Teasing us perhaps.

The warmth provides a false security that summer is

approaching

… soon.

The heat beats down simulating June weather.

I'm sure however that sneaky April may still surprise us

with her usual trick…

a sudden cold windy and damp spell

just to keep us on our toes.

Similar to life with its unexpected surprises.

I observe the small changes in nature

as metamorphosis takes place.

Change doesn't happen in a nanosecond

There's a process.

We need patience.

I breathe in the beautiful scene.

Nature mimics life

at its best

and at its worst.

Mostly we must work with,

focus on,

the gifts that nature brings us.

As we should do with life.

The slight breeze tickles my neck.

The lime green chartreuse shade of the newly budding trees

whose foliage will soon cover most of the condos

and street signs on the avenue,

brighten the path.

Splash!

A robin takes a dip in the pond

awakening the sedate life within.

Awakening my thoughts also.

Soon thereafter my first butterfly triad visit!

They dance around me before soaring higher

bringing me, as always,

messages from my angels.

I sit here listening to the words

that have been sent to me by my spirits.

These words empower, inspire, send messages to the

subconscious

encouraging me to continue to live with purpose.

I am not done serving.

I'm to keep dreaming bigger

despite my age

and despite all those that tell me

I should wind down.

Despite my adult kids who care about my health

But do not understand my need

to grow, give and glow.

I made a new expression today

for those who still feel unsatisfied.

I know you are out there,

those of you akin to me

knowing you can do more,

knowing you should do more,

but not knowing what.

Searching within yourself

as I do now,

Ask the following:

What's your real purpose?

Why are you still here?

What is your strength?

What can you offer others?

Your community?

The unfortunate?

The world?

Or simply your family or a loved one?

What is your gift?

Then ...

Shift to your gift!

Heed your own answers above and...

SHIFT TO YOUR GIFT

It's a beautiful thing.

ON TEARS

Release the tears and let them flow
Tears tell the tales, tears let them go
Don't be afraid, don't hold them back
Tears cry inside for what we lack
They are nature's hands to aid you through
Guiding cleansing, helping you
With relentless pain. Will it cease?
Tears lead you forth to clouds of peace
Cry angry tears out one by one
Set free them all until they're done
Shed tears of sadness; Let them flow
Breathe again, survive and grow
Dance once again! Pirouette once more!
For you've survived your personal war
Resilient now. The trauma freed
Fly now to where you are meant to be!

ABOUT THE POET

Vivian Shapiro is an energetic, positive-minded influencer, grateful to be active at 78 years! She is a best seller of both the co-authored ***Entangled No More*** and her own book, ***Go Vibrant! ...notes and anecdotes on loving and living the joie de VIVre.*** A Toronto teacher, VP, principal and charity Education Director, she spearheaded life changing programs to empower youth. She is a recipient of the 2012 *"Amazing Aces in Action Award"* and the 2018 *"Celebrating Outstanding Women Award for Philanthropy"* In her blended family, she is loved and known as "vava" to her thirteen grandchildren. With a passion to help one find the joy in living, she sees herself as the shining light to help be the spark for others.

Connect with Vivian below:

www.vivianshapiro.com/links

ABOUT THE PUBLISHER

International Best-Selling Author Katie Carey founded Soulful Valley Publishing House in 2021. Through her podcast and multi-author books, Katie helps metaphysical coaches, energy healers, authors, and creative business owners elevate their work. With a background in mental health advocacy, Katie blends science and spirituality to support mental, emotional, and physical wellbeing. Collaborating with like-minded individuals, Katie aims to bring these concepts to a wider audience. Contact Katie to collaborate on a multi-author book or write your own solo book.

Listen to Katie's Podcast Soulfulvalley below:

https://apple.co/3BkJdkn

Katie's Amazon Author Profile:

www.ingramcontent.com/pod-product-compliance
Lightning Source LLC
Chambersburg PA
CBHW071611040426
42452CB00008B/1311